OTHER BOOKS BY PETER MICHELSON

The Aesthetics of Pornography
The Eater
When the Revolution Really

PACIFIC PLAINSONG
I–XIII

Peter Michelson

*for David & Margie
who might like it
Peter*

Another Chicago Press
Chicago • 1987

Portions of *Pacific Plainsong* have appeared in the following: *New Poetry Anthology, The Eater, New Orleans Review, Chicago Review, Choice, The New Proteus, Sitting Frog,* and *TriQuarterly*.

Copyright © 1987 by Peter Michelson
All Rights Reserved.
ISBN (paper): 0-9614644-1-0
Library of Congress Catalog Card Number: 77-95077

Published in the United States by Another Chicago Press, Box 11223, Chicago IL 60611. Thanks to the Illinois Arts Council for financial assistance with this project. Originally published in 1978 by Brillig Works, Boulder, Colorado.

PREFACE TO THE FIRST EDITION

In its locomotives and foundries, its mines, fleets and bridges Walt Whitman heard America singing. "As nature," he said, "inexorable, onward, resistless . . . so America." Thus, in perfect faith and composure, " . . . we have not come through centuries, caste, heroisms, fables, to halt in this land today. . . . Let all defer. . . . Strangle the singers who will not sing you loud and strong. Open the doors of The West." And has this not, then, been in the American grain? Even in our hankering to shed Europe's skin have we not spoken from its soul . . . inexorable, onward, resistless? Who are we, we ineluctable heirs of destiny? And what other voices, "for there are always others," murmur in our celebrated idiom?

"From where the sun now stands," Chief Joseph said a hundred years ago, "I will fight no more forever." I would not redeem myself in Joseph's eloquence. Still, we have invoked ourselves in voices more remote by far. I do not, however, want it thought that this poem, *Pacific Plainsong,* laments injustice to the Indians. Still less that it should presume to speak for them. It speaks, in whatever frequency of stolen voices, of the moral logic endemic to our history with ourselves. "We may be brothers after all," said Chief Seattle, "we shall see."

Pacific Plainsong has been some while under way. Portions of it appeared in print in 1965, more in 1969, and more again in 1972, 1974 and 1976. Certain persons, over that decade and more, have been profoundly important to the poem's progress. While some have been publicly acknowledged, others have not. But they will know who they are. And they will know the depth of my appreciation. I wish also to thank the Swallow Press for its generous permission to reprint nearly half of this volume, Northwestern University for a grant enabling me to continue it, and the National Endowment for the Arts for granting me the time to complete it. And finally, my gratitude to Ron Pyke and Larry McKay of Brillig Works for the extraordinary dignity with which they have treated both me and *Pacific Plainsong.*

P. Michelson
February 1978

PHOTOGRAPHS

I
Indian Burial, 1884.
Photograph, by William E. Hook, courtesy of Colorado Historical Society.

II
Frances Densmore transcribing songs at the Bureau of American Ethnology, 1913, from unidentified Indian.
Photograph courtesy of Colorado Historical Society.

III
Annie Oakley and unidentified Indian.
Photograph, by David F. Barry, courtesy of Western History Department, Denver Public Library.

IV
Tommy Old Chief caddying for unidentified man, Glacier National Park.
Photograph, by Bob and Ira Spring, courtesy Glacier National Park, Inc.

V
Luther Standing Bear and William S. Hart.
Photograph, by David F. Barry, courtesy of Western History Department, Denver Public Library.

VI
Studio Burial.
Photograph, by David F. Barry, courtesy of Western History Department, Denver Public Library.

VII
Chief Joseph and William F. Cody shake hands at Wild West Show in Brooklyn.
Photograph courtesy of Mercaldo Archives.

VIII
Crow Mother, Baby No-Horse, and American Flag.
Photograph courtesy of Colorado Historical Society.

IX
Chief Hairy Chin, July 4, 1889, Bismark, North Dakota.
Photograph, by David F. Barry, courtesy North Dakota State Historical Society.

X
Tot Clifford and Chief Gall.
Photograph, by David F. Barry, courtesy of Western History Department, Denver Public Library.

XI
Sitting Bull and William F. Cody.
Photograph, by David F. Barry, courtesy Western History Department, Denver Public Library.

XII
Geronimo, his wife and children, in his melon patch, Fort Sill, Oklahoma, 1895-96.
Photograph courtesy of Museum of the American Indian, Heye Foundation.

XIII
Oglala Charley and Baptiste Pourier.
Photograph courtesy of Colorado Historical Society.

Dakota Burial.
Photograph, by David F. Barry, courtesy Western History Department, Denver Public Library.

I

Preface to *The Works* of H. H. Bancroft
Volume XXXI (History of Washington, Idaho, and Montana,
1845-1889)
pp. vi and vii

There were those determined to
serve not (as Vancouver) by
stepping on shore to luncheon and
reciting (ceremonies) to the
winds, nor by naming the
great River of the West for
(as Robert Gray had done)
his ship. There
were those who
served (as they determined) by
possessing there were those determined
servers determined (while securing to
themselves such homes as they might
choose) who by possessing
(of the territory) chose
to serve by taking there
were those who (by possession) chose
securely there such homes as
those (determined) who declining
luncheon and some ceremonies, chose
to serve and did (their
government) by taking territory
and (ceremonies to the winds) they
served by actual occupation.

I need not here repeat their
narrative I need not here

repeat those (bold) measures by
which these men of destiny their
destiny achieved. I
wish only to declare they
faced (those early pioneers) the
mystery, they faced the
great unknown—though (by whimsy, by
merest chance, or as we say
it fell out that) they
had found the choicest portions—
they had (of the great unknown)
found its fertile soil, its
wonderful inland sea, safe
from storms, always open to navigation,
abounding in fish, bordered
many miles wide with
the most magnificent forests on earth.

So (securing to themselves such
homes as they might choose) it
did (does) not require
a poet's vision to picture
a glowing future, albeit dim
in the reaches of time. And
to lay ever so humbly destiny's
cornerstone was worth the (humble)
toil and privation (abounding
in fish) the (safe from storms)
danger and the isolation (always
open to navigation) for
to lay destiny's cornerstone
(even) ever so humbly is worth it and
there were (weren't there)
among them those determined to serve.

Yes, and (incidentally)
this inland sea with

treasures inexhaustible of
food for the world and
fifteen hundred miles of shore covered
with pine forests to the
water's edge and
surrounding it small valleys of
the richest soils, watered
by streams from pure
snows of the Cascade
and Coast ranges, half prairie and half
forest, warm sheltered from winds enticing
the weary pilgrim from the eastern side
of the continent to rest in
their calm solitudes, so well did
God (and those who were determined to) serve

(though it was true that
the native wild man
still inhabited these valleys and
roamed the mountains to the number of
thirty thousand, the
incomers were sons of sires who
had met and
subdued the savage tribes of
America as they
pushed West from Plymouth Rock
to the Missouri and beyond—
therefore they had now no hesitation).

For bred to believe
that British and Indians would
melt before them they
(British and Indians melting before them)
had no hesitation and
(though there were among them
native wild men) they
(sons of savage sires) had

no hesitation and (bred to believe
in melting pots) they melted
British and Indians before
them and (determined
to serve) enticed weary pilgrims
to their calm solitudes for
there were (calm, determined) those
men of destiny facing
the great unknown there
were those bold those
determined who (securing to themselves
such as they might) chose
not (unrequired) a poet's
imagination (the British and Indians
melting) for among them were
the sons of sires determined
to serve and they (securing what
they chose) they had (picturing
a glowing future) they had therefore
(without ceremony) they had therefore now no hesitation.

The sources for this volume are those which have enabled me to write all my volumes.

II

"Today I met a rude, humble people . . .
scarcely better than animals . . . the
women busily engaged like swine, rooting
up the beautiful verdant meadow in
quest of wild onions . . ."
                    George Vancouver,   1792

          . . . a *people,* yes, but rude
              & humble, scarcely better—in
        fact in context—the equivalent of
                  swine . . . a rude &
              humble people, the equal of swine   animal
        unclean . . . *rude*   *rood* ME. AS. OFr. L.   akin to Gk.
            ME. AS. OFr. L.
                akin to Gk.   *rood* the dream
            of the rood . . . the passion
                    buried, obscure . . . the dream
                of the rude buried & obscure
              barbarous or ignorant: as, *rude* savages
              lacking refinement, culture, or elegance:
                  as, *rude* savages . . . harsh,
                discordant, not musical: as, *crude*
                    ME. AS. OFr. L. akin
            to Gk. bleeding, raw, akin to
                    cruor blood
                congealed, thickened, bloody
              akin to *cruel* . . . disposed
                    to inflict pain & suffering, to
                take delight therein: as,
            they are insolent, uncivil, crude, cruel, rude
                scarcely better nee equal to
                    swine . . . they take delight therein

> ... a *people,* yes, but humble
> & rude ... crude & cruel
> a relentless disregard for the rights & welfare
> of others ... the women
> like swine rooting
> the *verdant*
> meadows ... the women
> like swine rooting
> the *beautiful*
> meadows ... beautiful & verdant
> these Meadow Manors these Meadowbrook Hills the
> women like swine discordant
> rooting Elysian Fields ... barbarous, bloody
> raw, congealed ... giving
> birth beside the trail ... bloody
> inelegant swine, these
> are The Great Chain's missing link
> to be forged
> with relentless regard or disregard ...
> the fire burns
> insolent, uncivil, akin to L. akin to all
> we speak ... in or at one with
> neither grace nor generosity we are
> the heirs of arrogance set sail
> with the gift of fire, with
> the advantage of Greek ...
> we take delight therein ...
>
> ... a people, yes, but rude
> & *humble humilis*
> akin to *humus* ... the soil
> the earth ... lowly
> lacking refinement ... taking delight therein
> *humus, humilis* the soil, the earth:
> as, a humble people
> rooting the earth, taking
> delight therein ...

humus humilitas humanus humanitas
   akin to man akin
      to earth . . . engaged
  like swine
     amid the verdant meadows
    amid abundant forests
      amid the navigable inland seas . . .
humilitas humanitas humilitas in
   quest of wild onions I
  met today a rude & humble people
  humanus humanitas humaine humayne
akin to *cruor* akin to blood akin to birth . . . beside
   the trail, there
    was no wonder at the birth
        or blood . . .
 Whom do you seek, O swine of the field?
  humus humilitas humanus humanitas
   the dream the dream of the
  dream of the rood the dream of the rood is
    buried deep . . .
  akin to earth akin
     to man . . . *cruor* crude
cruor rude ME. AS. OFr. L. akin to Gk.
Whom, O swine of the field,
    Whom do you seek?
  who placed us here is here . . .
we come from no country . . . and what we seek . . .
   the dream
  of the rude . . . *humilitas* in quest
 of wild onions . . . *humanitas* to
      take delight therein . . .
a sow's ear in a silk purse
   today I met a people
  The Great Chain's missing link
to forge   relentless
   regard or disregard: as
 at My Lai we are under orders

   certified sane
      in all respects . . .
   humilitas   the fire burns
     humanitas   the fire burns
  sane
in all respects regard or disregard
  relentless Whom, O scarcely more
than swine, do you seek? O Whom
     uncivil inelegant people . . .
  humanitas humanitas humanitas
   . . . we are here
   uncivil inelegant people
    engaged like swine
rooting the beautiful meadow in quest of Whom
   O people . . .
      humilitas humilitas
   . . . we are
  the heirs of arrogance set sail
   with the gift of fire, with
  the advantage of Greek . . .
     hybris hybris
    under orders
     certified sane
   we take delight therein . . .

III

Plainsong at Lapush

Locked in locked
in this (neither past nor
present) anachronistic village is
shrouded in its battered sea
spray air—its shoreline stacked
with stoney bleached enormous (two
feet thicker than
a man is tall) carcasses
of trees, their jagged roots upended
claw the (sullen) sky—all
all is shroud and bonewhite gleaming
along this brittle shore.

A (well past bearing) squaw
rocks amid the baskets she
no longer weaves and looks beyond the mist
bound shore complaining men no longer ride
the open boats or
risk rough water out at sea.
In the village (white) Mark
Westby teaches Indians (one or two) their
ancient craft of carving—offshore
Shell Oil blasts leviathan
and salmon, sounding lively
messages of profit through this pall
of spray. But I came to see
fishers at their trade, and
their past a curio,
their present obsolete

I watch the ghosts of Kwakiutl,
oil skinned and glistening, astride
the pitch and swell, they
work their dark pacific
sea and bend to haul up gleaming
nets, to bring rich flesh
of fish to air; their
calloused fingers slap the
gaff deep in the heaving
gills they snare—implacably
they gaff that signal writhing, gaff
and know an old despair.

IV

Leschi's Mad Song

(From Telstar) camera pans
whole of continental U.S., at
Seattle zooming to
intersection of Yesler Street (original skid
road) with Elliot Bay waterfront to
(chief) Leschi, then, wearing Brando/Zapata
expression of (profound)
ennui and dedication, standing at
corner—fish trucks, tourists, and
stevedores in background, as
Mac and Muff (teeny boppers) play
(discrete) grabass, watching jellyfish
orgasm in the bay. All is
tranquil and godfearing
bustle of enterprise when
Leschi (in war paint, headress, and bear's
tooth necklace) shakes
a tambourine and bellows, "White Mother
fuckers," then (having just the night
before seen Sammy Davis Jr. as a t.v. cavalry
sergeant) adds, "Black Mother
fuckers!" All freeze agape (except Mac in slight
grimace as Muff, freezing, catches his
foreplay digit in sphincter
lock), Leschi begins war
dance, chanting Nisqually
medicine ("The times they are
achangin," punctuated at
grace notes with lyrical *White*
and/or *Black Muahfu*) and
prancing about intersection plunging

a harpoon through tires and
denting hoods and fenders with
tomahawk. All freeze until traffic cop comes
to and shouts "All right, Mac, cut it!"
(Mac, misunderstanding, looks up
terrified, frantically doubling
efforts at digitus
interruptus from rigid Muff), Leschi
ignoring cop continues his demonic
attack on Yesler and waterfront. The cop
unable to solicit help, as
all hold freeze, launches into "Indian
Love Call" which awakens Muff (much
to Mac's relief), who is
in real life a beautiful octoroon Nisqually
princess studying voice at Cornish
School and she (loving men in
uniform) responds with Kundry's seduction
aria from "Parsifal" which
baffles cop until they get together in
duet of "God Bless America (and nobody
else.)" They exit (after encores) to
an emergency cop phone and call
the riot squad which
comes and pounds Leschi (who continues throughout
chanting and prancing oddly about banging,
poking with tomahawk and harpoon until
subdued) to Burgerchef tenderized consistency, as
camera pans from business-as-usual at
Yesler and waterfront while the traffic cop is
locked with Muff in an inarresting sex
arrangement, as (close-up)
jellyfish undulate in bay.

Scene two opens in courtroom, as
prosecutor concludes, ". . . from every
lamppost, by the good Lord above we'll

have law and order in this
land." The jury goes
berserk, foreman grabs up a flag, others
produce fife and drum, all march and sing "Yankee
Doodle" around the courtroom. Spectators remain
calm though fuddled. As Public Defender
shrieks, "My client, even though a filthy, backward
savage, pleads not guilty, but
personally I wasn't at the scene of
the crime so
it's hard for me to say."
Jury starts up again but judge
gestures hypnotically with
outstretched palm. "What," he asks
Leschi, "have *you* to say?"
Leschi gestures hypnotically (gives
judge the finger) and shouts *White Mother
fucker;* sees a black cop, *Black Mother
fucker!* Cop keeps stoneyphizz but
straightens smart black leather
cravat and adjusts smart black leather
ammo holster belt, resting
hand on revolver butt, eyes
smiling *Man it more blessed
to give (shit) than receive (it)—
every motherfucker for himself*
(sings "Ol' Man River").
Public Defender interjects to
(bug-eyed, outraged) judge
"My client means this
whole thing is mistaken, he's
just an actor studying his
role on the street, but
personally I wasn't at the scene of
the crime so
it's hard for me to say."

Pandemonium again, until
Prosecutor cries, "Objection, his
act's too good, Yesler Street's no
stage for pissant players to
buggar traffic while
they hone their mocking
methods . . . We're witness here
to muckrakery and (reason)
treason spreading *seeds* throughout the land. I
call on witnesses to (lie)
testify: this bad good actor's stopped
up traffic . . . *He whomped my hood, Dented
my truck, Was up to no
good, Why he said fuck!* Too
much! The judge leaps up shrieking, "If
niggers can by God learn not to
shit in corridors and keep
a tight zipper on their fly (black
cop covertly checks his) then
you stinking savages can learn to
live like Christians (jury
cheers, spectators, still calm and
fuddled, applaud) and (by God) you're GUILTY
GUILTY GUILTY and we'll (by
God) make you all good (dead)
injuns or know the (by God) reason
why" (Jury foreman leads "locomotive"
for Law and Order) as
(from Telstar) camera pans whole
of continental U.S. and
orchestra overlays muted "America
the Beautiful" on electronic reverberations of
Everett Dirkson reciting (in
unctuo) *with liberty and justice for all* . . . as
Leschi goes to gallows

and ". . . on the 19th of
February the unhappy
savage,
ill and emaciated
from long confinement and
weary of a life which
for nearly three years had been
one
of strife
and misery, was
strangled
according to law."
strangled according to law
the law according to
which he strangled
was law
(according to law)
and he was strangled
according to perhaps not his
law
but according to some (which?)
law
he was strangled and
according(ly)
he
dangled
from and jerked about (dares
Justice jerk her lovers off)
the gallows (?) That
act's tough to follow, but
before "a large concourse of people (there) assembled"
he (weary) according(ly)
according to some
perhaps not his
law he
(an emaciated method
actor studying the lead

for his own life
story) was
strangled
according was
strangled according to law.

Though few chiefs survived it and
"His (Leschi's) death may be said to
have been the closing act of
the war on Puget Sound,"
"Kissass (stet) Kussass, chief
of the Cowlitz, (lived)
114 years. He
was friendly, and a Catholic."

V

"Seattle is described as a dignified and venerable personage, whose carriage reminded the western men of Senator Benton; but I doubt if the Missouri senator would have recognized himself . . . in this naked savage who conversed only in signs and grunts."

                Sealth, your brazen
         image labors now beneath the
           bowels of pigeons, or
          now and then a gull will
         bring you tidbits from the
       bay. Your moulded eyeballs gaze
        on produce of the land you've
     vanished from—at this postcard skid
road square, at tourists, sailors, cops, sullen
         Indians, and reeking Yesler
bums. Chief, my (suburban) youth was fed on
        myths of your (pacific)
wisdom. Our ancestors loved you (we were
       told) and named their town for
you. You weren't (like Kitsap) pushy or
      (like Leschi) mad. You knew
your place. And (footnotes to your history say) you
  taxed the settlers (shrewdly) for these restless
       nights you walk, your ghost
    unearthed by (chatty) invocations of
      your name. That fraud vindicates a
    savage (naked) born and remnant to
       the Age of Reason. You
learned the game. History footnotes (at least) a man
     who bites a dog or an injun who
      screws a white man without
    contracting clap. Counsellor, even

though (poor bastard) you didn't have the
style of a (Missouri) senator, you
counselled well to keep your tribe from
war. The Dwamish fished
in peace, were dry and warm in
winter, and died a quiet
death. They
extinguished themselves with dignity. Knowing
your (civic) duty, you merchandised
your cosmos to these states. So
now I come to see your (memorial)
reward, to Yesler where your noble profile
sits, your
brazen headress gleaming
in the rain, and
your stern (prophetic) glare ignores
the shoulder (twitching) where
a balding eagle shits.

Nor mountain no
nor bronze nor
stone are monument
gargantuan howevermuch
enough

Though Crazy
Horse
emerge at last from South
Dakota hills, his
mountain blasted tombstone's
pork barrel boondoggle
DRAG
show, *(See Folks, step up, look close—*
beneath the Breechclout,
stone)

A concrete buffalo three
storeys high gazes
down a North
Dakota draw, hot
for cows that never
come
gargantuan howevermuch
enough.

Air ripper, jack
hammer, blast, beam, and
balls we shape
Mohammed in the mountain, lament and
scan the edge of earth: such
remembering—poem, plate, or
song—is molding
making all horizons take
cadavered shape.

Emerge at last though
Crazy Horse he
may from South Dakota hills his
ghost is
friendly.
(Him good injun)

Custer died for your sins
says redskin bumper wit.
But vestigial Sitting Bull, amused,
knows more precisely who wins,
how little the sea churns
or earth burns to pay for sins.
When Joseph, who survived White Bird Canyon,
Big Hole and Absaroka,
survived the treachery of Assiniboines and Crow,
was hounded thirteen hundred miles by Sherman's Army,
haunted by starvation, cold, spectres of extinction,

When Joseph sent to Sitting Bull for help
he (the Custer killer) said
Joe, do you, like Crazy Horse, expect some miracle from these hills?
You might as well piss upstream
to keep water from the dam—
give up, man,
Custer was a bad scene from a (B) flick—
but the ultimate (comedian) is Uncle Sam.
No matter how the sea churns
or earth burns to pay for sins
the guy that lasts is the one who wins.

In 1866 old Seattle watched
the sun, at Alki, extinguish, ripple orange, warm and
conjure sachems, their shimmer, his eyes, visions,
shimmer trails behind the sun—Seattle, tired
and prophetic in his impotence, saw old ghosts (no
ghosts) ghosts in '66. He learned
from Jesuits, and mad Leschi's execution, to
read graffiti on statehouse (outhouse) walls.

Nor mountain no
nor bronze nor
stone are monument
gargantuan howevermuch
enough

Seattle, this naked savage who conversed in signs and grunts, says to President Polk:
Day and night cannot live together. The red man has ever run before the white man, as morning mist before the morning sun. But your proposition seems fair. My people will accept the reservation. We will live apart in peace. The words of the white chief are the words of nature speaking to my people, speaking out of a dense darkness. . . .
It matters little where we pass the remnant of our days—they

will not be many. A few more moons, a few more winters . . . tribe follows tribe, and nation nation like the waves of the sea— that is nature's order. Regret is useless. Your decay may be distant, but it will surely come. Even the white man whose God walked and talked with him as friend with friend cannot deny his destiny. We may be brothers after all. We shall see. . . .

    (this land is ours
   or yours your ships your
    cavalry confirm
    the stars are sky is
  dark our visions dark our
    gods gone your
    god grins your
  cavalry your ships confirm
     his grin it
   matters little where
  we pass our days your
guns diminish gods your grinning
    cavalry confirms
    it little matters I
    shall not mourn I
    shall forget my
     god I
  shall sign your deed this
   land is my tribe is
blood this land is graves holy
ashes holy land is mine is
    sacred ours
     or yours
your cavalry your gods and dead
leave their land or graves wander
  fields beyond the sun our
  dead remain their dust is
   rich with blood white
  man the dead are bloody

dust white
man the dead are dust
dust prevails our
dust we bathe
bloody our visions white
man you will never be
alone be just
remember blood the
dust is not without its power.)

In the morning fog off Alki in the bay
Decatur's cannon prowls.
Dolphins arc before her dripping prow,
and from the sky
gulls crash clams against
the indifferent shore's rewarding stone.

Nor mountain no
nor bronze nor
all the elegies of man are
monument gargantuan howevermuch
enough

VI

"Though coming to them under color of peace, it was charged upon the chief that he intended to entrap them. However this may have been,

            the volunteers, not content with
           putting so powerful an enemy out of
the way, amused themselves that evening in camp by
           cutting off bits of his scalp as
           trophies; and when the scalp was
           entirely gone, the assistant surgeon of
           the regiment cut
           off his ears,
           and it was said some
           of his fingers . . .
           Parrish probably exaggerates
           when he says: They
           skinned him from head to
           foot, and made razor-straps of
           his skin."
           He (Parrish) probably
           exaggerates. For it's unlikely that
the head, hands, or feet could be skinned
efficiently, the best incision (easiest) being to
           cut from the neck base splaying
down the spine bypassing the rectum (arcing right
and left) across smooth buttock blubber to
the scrotum (keeping the tool flaccid and ground-
           ward, the Indians so far as we
know being the first American sister and mother
fuckers), continue the seam down the inside of each
           thigh to the ankle, encircling incisions around
           ankles, privates, arms (usually not
           worth their hide, excepting extraordinary

biceps) and neck, then simply peel
hide from carcass (being careful
about the ribs) and stretch to cure—though I
should note that of all skins
the human is suited more for ornamental
than productive purposes, and will not
strop a razor well, so he (Parrish) probably
exaggerates. The volunteers (perhaps) amused
themselves with bits of scalp and ears and
(it was said) some fingers, but most certainly
he (Parrish) goes too far in saying they
made razor-straps of skin. And
though the volunteers were enter-
prising men they (after all) were
men and Waiilatpu in December is
not (even today) an amusing place and
as the Walla Walla girls weren't (it may be
supposed) putting out to the enemy
the Oregon yankees (resourcefully)
amused themselves in camp, though
it would exaggerate to say they (like
Shriners) went too far and surely he (Horace
Greeley) exaggerates (like Parrish) to
say (in 1858), "The enterprising territories of Oregon
and Washington have handed into congress their
little bill for scalping Indians and violating
squaws" for (as history records) truth must beware
exaggeration and most certainly they
bleed too much who say those
volunteers excessively amused
themselves in camp with
bits of scalp and ears and (it was
said) some fingers

"Thus perished the wealthy and powerful chief of the Walla Wallas."

VII

Centenary Sequence for the Dreamers

1

About suffering they knew little more
than anybody else, the ancients
and old masters. Tragedy, said one,
is imitation. He was wrong.
Tragedy, as he like the other also
knew, is when you choose—or don't—to drink
the hemlock. And questions of art are, we say
these days all too unwittingly, questions
of execution. So, we find, are those
of life. Questions of art, then, are questions
of life—matters, that is, of execution.
And after suffering, no matter whose,
we would not be purged. They taught us wrong
those who sought the laws. Ask him who chose
the hemlock or him who told the tale.

2

Knowing depravity from Calvin
old Marc Whitman must have
died smiling, as a
jagged Cayuse hatchet jellied
his relentless brain . . . One
hundred years prove
he didn't smile
in vain. This happy
valley reeks with God's
inexorable plan, his

grace: here
Whitman came with
Calvin's god and small
pox malignantly in
hand; with Augustine's heart
burnt cork he smeared
alien stone
age souls, he
dipped their well
pocked bodies in this
valley's many waters—at
Walla Walla vestigial un-
elected savages atoned
grim souled Swiss or
rare Babylonian
sins . . .

Waiilatpu, place of
rye grass, once
ground for this
valley's native councils,
now it honors
Whitman, his
mission and his
kin. His hilltop
monument tapers to the
sky—a finger gesturing
abuse, enshrined, officiously
fenced in. Down
the hill, across
a road, beyond
the mission's old
foundations, a rutted creek
bed commends the Nez Perce,
Walla Walla and
Cayuse, drained long
since and dead . . .

3

It is the soul of things the thing's soul
whatever it may be the soul of
we must discover. And can. There are
arguments in history worth hearing.
We do what we can, though some say *must* and others
will. Nonetheless, we do. And poetry
among them is not much. We may agree
on that. Yet, as the Dr. said, every
day we die for lack of what is found
there. True, the state of gods is not what
it was . . . Likewise authority, and magicians
among us now are entertainers. Still
one quite lately says, "I am not
an entertainer," putting us on our mettle.
It is hard work for us, this talking . . . like
heavy lifting it buzzes in our heads . . .
too heavy lifting every day, said Yellow Wolf . . .

4

Smoholla the Dreamer's Song

My young men shall never work
For men who work can never dream
My young men shall never work
For men who work can never dream
And wisdom comes to us in dreams
And wisdom comes to us in deams

Sa'ghalee Tyee   Sa'ghalee Tyee
Show me what is in your heart
Show me what is in your heart
I will tell them all
I will tell them all about it

Sa'ghalee Tyee made the red man first
He made the red man first
The Chinaman who sews and irons
The Chinaman with a tail
The Chinaman who sews and irons
The Chinaman He made last
All the rest . . . the Frenchman and the priest
The Boston men King George's men all the white men and the black
All the rest are in between
He made the red man first
They were called the people
They were called the people
And like the eagle He gave the red man wings

On these shores grew many people
And the strong oppressed the weak
Sa'ghalee was angry   He took away their wings
On these shores grew many people
And the strong oppressed the weak
Sa'ghalee was angry   He took away their wings
He said the lands were common   And the fishes in the sea
Sa'ghalee was angry
He said the lands were common   And the fishes in the sea

Sa'ghalee is the father and earth the mother of man
Yet the white man tells me *plow the ground*
Shall I take a knife and tear my mother's breast?
And the white man tells me *quarry stone*
Shall I dig beneath her skin for bones?
The white man tells me *make hay be rich* like him
How dare I cut and sell my mother's hair?
Sa'ghalee is the father and earth the mother of man
Sa'ghalee is angry   His people deny the law
Sa'ghalee is angry   He makes the white man strong
He does not love them those who sell their lands
He does not love them those who buy and sell the land

We freely take His gifts
As they are freely offered
And no more harm the earth
Than would an infant's fingers
Harm its mother's breast

But the white man cuts and tears   He scars our mother earth
The white man cuts and tears   He scars our mother earth
And calls this work his mission
His soul is hard with work
He calls this work his mission
And Doctor Whitman says we sin
His mission mutilates our mother
Bringing poison and disease
His mission kills our children
And his medicine is sin
But the white man tears the prairies
And the white man gouges forests
And mutilates the body of our mother
He drives stakes into her bosom
He marks it off in squares
And calls this work his mission
With work the white man's soul is hard
His mind diseased with sin

Sa'ghalee is angry and earth the mother of man
Sa'ghalee is angry
He said the lands were common
And the fishes in the sea
He will drive away the people
Excepting those who keep the law
He will drive away the people
Excepting those who keep the law

Come Sa'ghalee to the center here
where I live   in my heart
I set my feet upon this mother earth

I set my heart upon the great north star
That star ever in its place
I keep my heart upon that star

He will drive away the white man   back across the sea
He will drive away the white man   back across the sea
Our mother earth is slashed and torn
Sa'ghalee will make her new
The people and the creatures
Sa'ghalee will make her new
The people and the creatures
Sa'ghalee will make us new

As the left hand slides across the right
He will make the earth anew
As the left hand slides across the right
He will make the earth anew

The dead
The dead are coming
The dead are coming to sing with us
The dead are coming to smoke the salmon
The dead are coming and once again the buffalo
Our sons are coming to sing with us
Our daughters coming to dance with us
Our mothers coming to pray with us
Our fathers coming to beat the drums
My people are
Over the whole earth
My people are coming again
Over the whole earth my people are coming
Over the whole earth the red man and the law
The eagle tells me
The eagle tells me

And my young men shall never work
For men who work can never dream
And my young men shall never work
For men who work can never dream

5

Among us those who choose. As we step
up to the bar, the barkeep, resplendent in
his handlebar mustache, his sleeves bloused
by red silk garters, or sometimes sporting black
robes and judicial airs, the barkeep,
always affable and adroit, smiling
says, *All right, Gents, name your poison.*
And smiling back, we choose. Graciously
we toss the man a tip. *Buy yourself
a drink,* we say. He deftly scoops the spinning
coin from midair and tests its purity
against his teeth. His teeth indent the soft
rich gold. Smiling, he pockets the coin. The truth
is this: *he doesn't drink, he only pours . . .*
As if, said Joseph, *a man should come to me
and say, I like your horses, I want to buy them.
I say No, my horses suit me, I will
not sell. He goes to my neighbor and says, Joseph
has good horses . . . I want to buy them but
he will not sell. My neighbor answers, Pay me
the money, and I will sell you Joseph's horses.*
Affable and adroit the barkeep changes
guise . . . but, in whatever guise he goes
his sleeves are bloused for business. So, we choose.
And yet, we drink precisely what he pours.
Clever Lawyer, changes guise, and learns
to mix a drink. . . . He was a man, as one
might say, of exquisite understanding, one
who was a Christian, one who learned the laws . . .

6

Is the story, then, too simple
for our own exquisite tastes? We
speak not here of noble
savages nor of their romance. This
story, though often told, has been projected
so transpicuous its plot must thicken
into mush. And it is after all
the lucid soul of things the
thing's soul whatever
it may be the soul of
we must discover. And can.
For matters of art, like life, are
matters of execution, and if
we would have the cause we
must go back. There
are arguments in history worth hearing . . .
●

We must go back, remember it?
as we were taught, Phoenicians
selling nuclear can openers with Kabbalist
instructions coded into alphabet soup,
a free speed-reading course in every bowl,
remember it? the fruits of
enterprise . . .
●

And the grandeur? circuses, highways
and aquaducts still standing, laws,
Christians, and commerce spread like water
to all reaches of empire, the fasces
much admired still, and Christians
even then granting what's his (or yours)
to Caesar . . .
●

And the glory, remember it? Athens, where
everyone, stripped to the waist, would work

the fields, keeping stoneyphizzed
at even *Dagmar's* tits, says Socrates,
swaying above the hoe, and
we all have upward mobility excepting
slaves of course, who are quite worthless, remember it?
the love of Truth, disinterested . . . Socrates and
the barkeep discoursing, even as he drinks,
of Truth and State . . . dying already in his belly
he is glad, this model citizen, to do his part,
as Athenians, said Pericles before the bier,
are yet more worthy since enlarging
their own inheritance into *empire*
extensively bequeathed to us their sons . . .

•

If after suffering we would not be purged
we must go back, declining
ancient draughts and bromides
we vulgarians who came to conquer
and stayed to learn, remember it? as we were taught
the critics of it, Gibbon even, smug
and securely . . . Mediterranean,
we must go back
        to?
      O Brave New World!
        Elizabeth and Isabella picking up the pieces
  of empire . . .

•

handing them to the fathers . . . Adams, remember it?
praising Athens and Rome, *powers* he called them,
for having "honored our species
more than all the rest . . ." Meanwhile
George Washington, throwing a silver dollar west
across the Potomac, winked and said, shrewdly,
"Stay out of foreign wars . . ."
"By which he meant," said Quincy, a chip
off the old block any way you chisel,
"It seems the very will of *Providence*

that this entire continent be inhabited
by one people, but, since *Providence* (*God* wouldn't
melt in his empirical mouth) helps those
who help themselves, by all means stay
out of foreign wars . . . let's
keep our eye on the ball . . ."
>
> *I have done nothing*
> *for their teaching, these*
> *savages, they will not*
> *listen and prate of the land*
> *our mission tithes from them . . .*
> *and of the pox . . .*
> *They are diseased*
> *and the hand of Providence*
> *removes them to give place*
> *to a people more worthy*
> *of this fertile country . . .*

So Spaulding, Whitman . . . which? the barkeep
everywhere adroit conducts the Hallelujah
chorus, making the world safe for Providence
& Enterprise, Ltd., bigger
than the Hanseatic League Rothschilds Krupp or
Caesar himself Grandaddy to General
Motors the great neo-Platonic synthesis
of God and man
in a Rube Goldberg Whirlygig
raising Commerce from the muck
of its own jackboots
to sit with Him hip by haunch blowing
the very Will of Providence blood
rushing to His obelisk stone hard
with Destiny and Determination most
tremendous tool—opposable thumb and mathematics
notwithstanding—in the pornographic history
of the west. "And say what you will,"
said Buffalo Bill adjusting Joseph's bonnet
in the Hippodrome, "the Big Boy

sure knows how to use it . . ."
                          •
Musical chairs, change metaphor, think
Levittown Shaker Heights Webster Grove Anaheim Louisiana
      Purchase the Phillipines
      think *real estate*
      the new world
      suburb to ye olde
the ethos
laissez faire, remember it? bootstraps
opportunity keep your nose clean keep it
to the grindstone time
is money laissez faire, remember it?
as we were taught and made imago
Horatio Alger J. P. Morgan John Jacob Astor Howard Hughes (who
brought us suppliant and dripping in
their lobster grip Russian tuna disguised
as submarines *plus,* succulent
and dripping, Jane Russell's magnificient pout
and cleavage, for a roll in the hay
with Sergeant York and Lance Allworthy, "There,"
says the Voice of America, "*that* ought to hold
the little bastards," and it does it holds us
we love it absolutely
love it . . .

          (this diatribe in fact brought to you
by a grant from Exxon simulcast with "Revelooshunairey Revels"
rock opera starring Marx Lenin
Trotsky Mao Castro and Sun Yat-sen, the
Castrati Chorale, brought to you uninterrupted
because
          there is nothing absolutely
          nothing to fear) so

precociously suburbanite are we
to an upbeat Mediterranean, our

future even now dependent
on the European Common Market, "What
you feared as the Yellow Peril," says Mao
truckin' with the Greek
generals, "you will come to know as the Yellow Sun
of your well being . . ." we

must go back, the virus
as Burroughs said it would
is spreading . . .

7

Dakotah Dreamsong

In Dakotah the Standing Bears the Kicking Birds
the Young-Men-Afraid-of-their-Horses lie down,
alone, where the great plains
slope to rivers—Big Horn, Musselshell, Missouri . . .
And all around them
sky, sky and earth
and the creatures thereof . . . they are one
with the eagle and the mouse
among the hip-high grasses, here
where the great plains slope to rivers
they lie down, alone, at dusk
beneath the Moon-of-the-Geese-Gathering . . .

In the dreams they dream great
flights of geese wheel
in the morning light . . . their breasts gleam,
flashing black and silver
signals from above the rising autumn sun . . .
With each tremendous arcing turn,
like immense arrowheads in the sky,
from north and east and west, they come . . . ghostly

silent apparitions drawn inexorably
to the living wheel, in the Month
of the Gathering of the Geese . . .

When at last they wake
the young men wake to light
more splendid still
than aureoles of August moons, their
very act of waking, mediation,
so stunning is this canopy of arctic lights . . .
They lie still, wide-eyed
beneath basilica more brilliant
than the galaxies . . . Around them
neither owl nor coyote move,
caught by incandescence in
the arching ribs of rare Dakotah nights . . .
Here, where great plains slope
to rivers, are young men more graced
than in their birth . . . and wake
as if to silver geese auroral
in effulgent flight . . . here
where waters of the river stop,
giving back upon itself the sight
young men purify themselves to see,
light and light and light
climbing the holy arch of night . . .

8

". . . as if a
completely new race of man were," Jonas
says, "emerging. Do you know what
The Byrds do with their money? They are
making huge signs and putting them along
the roadsides of California, and the signs
say one word: Love. That's where we stand

in 1966." Think about it.
Jonas says, consider *The Byrds* . . .
make roadsigns saying *Love.* Roadsigns. Love.
The Byrds. A completely new race emerging.
The Byrds. Make roadsigns love and money. Hmmmm . . .
Farmers need the rent. Foster and Kleiser
need the work. "Where are we *now*—the underground?"

●

This is exordium . . . this
is figura . . . exordium/figura . . . fine words, do
we know what they mean? We will know
whereof they speak . . . precisely. We are all tired
of fine words that come to nothing . . .
Exordium . . . Figura . . . Exordium Exordium Exordium
already it is taking shape
in our mouths . . . exordium
    we will know
    exordium
    we are all tired

●

the hands of Providence are diseased
and prate of mission
giving place
to a fertile pox
more worthy of these savages . . .
They are diseased, the hands
of Providence. Remove them.
Listen, they are diseased . . .

9

Joseph's Song

 I am Hinmatoo Yahlatlat, *Joseph,* I
 heard the thunder rolling I
 counselled peace we

were as deer white
men the grizzly you
call me Joseph I
heard the thunder rolling (the
Earth is mother
of all and wisdom
comes in dreams) let
things remain white man
as they were made are
you white man the world's maker did
you make the sun? or
the grass to grow? as
well expect the rivers white
man to run backward as
that any man born free be otherwise
contented you
go where you please you
are not nor I
a child I am tired
of talk good
words that come to nothing Lawyer
Lawyer Lawyer white man there
has been too much
talk by men who had
no right to talk Hear
me my chiefs if
ever we owned our land we
own it still the
Earth is mother of all This
I believe my people believe
the same if *ever* . . .
we own it still as I
am Hinmatoo Yahlatlat hereafter
men may call me Joseph men
may call me wise
and brave and good but
I am tired of war I

counselled peace our
chiefs are killed White
Bird with Sitting Bull it's
cold we
have no blankets children
freeze my people in
the hills my children dying Hear
me I counselled peace Hear
me my heart is sick Hear
me white man as well
expect the rivers running backward white
man though you have won as
well expect the rivers to
run back as make a man contented
who is not free Hear
me white man as I hear you the
Earth is mother of all Hear
me white
man as you move the mountains Earth
white man is mother and
wisdom comes
in dreams it's
cold our children cold our
chiefs are dead Hear
me Hear me my chiefs from
where the sun now stands I
will fight no more
forever Hinmatoo Yahlatlat
has spoken for his people

VIII

Fourth of July Oration

    My fella Mericans, you know me, I've
spoke to you before. I
        am the eater, I consume.
           Thirty times my weight
in food, good MERICAN food—
United Fruit, Armour beef, Swift's pork, McDonald's ham-
    burgers, Purina
  wheat, barley, corn and soy beans . . .
      2,500 times
my weight in goods—General
        Motors, Sears
washers, RCA stereos, Weyerhaeuser lumber, Portland
        cement, Goodyear tires . . . And
two times my income annually in services—
  mortgages, loans, credit cards . . . You
      know me, MERICANS,
  I'm, *one* of ya . . .
      And, my fella MERICANS,
  I'm here to tell ya
    that the state of the union
is terrific. I mean, praise be, we're *Number One!*
  We started small, as
befits a prudent, hardworkin people. But
  we kept a good credit ratin, our
noses clean and to the grindstone,
    and today, this day of days, we
got somethin to show.
Somethin, MERICANS, to be *proud* of.
    MERICANS,
  this whole fuckin continent is *ours!*
      Yes MERICANS,

and the free world too!
And don't you worry none about them Commies, pinkos, and
fella travelers, MERICANS,
the Reds are on the run. The
Chinks buy our airplanes and
the Rooskies buy our wheat. Don't
you worry about that, MERICANS,
we got em by the balls.
We handled the Redskins (nod
of acknowledgment here
to the chiefs seated on the platform,
feathered and buckskinned,
led by a mannikin on loan
from the Department of the Interior's
Museum of Good Indians) we
handled the Redskins and
WE'LL HANDLE THE REDS!

MERICANS, we kept the faith, the
simple and effective
faith of our fathers: whatever
mother you can, cream him.
Anybody else,
mek a deeal! (for
only a little down and, yes,
less than a lifetime a month I
can put you behind the wheel
of a seventeen hundred and seventy-
six horse power E Pluribus Mirabulus
GRAND PRIX! So
come on in, Gringo
come on in to your old Uncle Sam's.
*You wont find
another deal in town.* And
remember this, my fella MERICANS, at
your old Uncle Sam's, *you*

   cut the cards: if
     you turn up an ace, *we*
       pay the freight! Yessirreebob,
   it's the old acey-deucy,
        a little game of chance
   with your Uncle Sam . . . be
       the first to win . . . hurry,
Hurry, HURRY . . . time
   is rapidly drawin to a close!)

     But I don't mean to say
that everything is peaches and
       frijoles (nod of acknowledgment here
to the wetback contingent, also
seated on the speaker's platform, led
     by mannikin of a barefoot Cesar
Chavez with a *wooden* lettuce knife, you
can't be too
    careful) No
     Sir, MERICANS, we
   still got us a job to do. Because,
      my fella citizens, sad
     though it is to say, there's
  bellyachers and troublemakers, yess, my
fella MERICANS, troublemakers and bellyachers.
   Yeaah, after all our work and
sacrifice to make this country what it is today,
    we still got us a job to do! Just
  listen, fella citizens, listen a moment:
     what do ya hear?
   Nothin, right? NOTHIN! *That,*
ladies and gents, is the work of the bellyachers.
  This is the Fourth of July, Independence
  Day, we
    ought to be hearin *explosions,*
     FIREWORKS,

    that's what we ought to hear!
Fireworks is what this country is about, my fella
  MERICANS. Fireworks! But
    out here on the reservation,
on guvmint propity, my fella MERICANS,
    almost no firecrackers are bein
    (ladies beggin your pardon) *blown!*
    Now the average for 'breeds in the cities
is slightly higher, but
     the deficiency is alarmin.
  My fella MERICANS, this
     is serious. We're
  harborin, at guvmint expense, with
the tax dollars you and me have sweated for, with
the giveaway, the welfare state, and the dole, we're
  harborin right here on these reservations
    bellyachers and unAMERICANS.

   Just this mornin, right here on Redapple Reservation,
over at that beautiful new motel designed and furnished by
    Dupont hisself, that
  motel we loaned em the money for
   at only 28% per annum per diem, I
was askin that pretty little redskin clerk (like
   to get her out behind the old earth-lodge, eh
  MERICANS!) I asks her
   for the mornin paper. She
    says, pert as you please, "They
     ain't deliverin today." So
   I says, friendly and humorous like, I says,
"Chuckle, chuckle," I says, "no good news *today.*"
And, my fella MERICANS, that sassy little bitch (Oh
  gawd, just five minutes behind the barn!)
    she looks me straight in the eye
   and she says, *Must be the Fourth of July!*
That's what we're up against: *smart-ass unAMERICANS!*

          Now the question is,
       what're we gonna do about it.
      True, we could hunt em down and
            root em out, but,
    pardners, we already done that. And
            the truth is, we need our ammunition.
         Yeaah, we got the Reds on the run, but
   you can't never tell about those little *yella* people.
         The Bolsheviks don't even trust em.
            No, my fella MERICANS,
       we got to keep our powder dry. Here
       on the home front there's other tactics,
    tactics we learned bringin peace to Ve-et-naam.
          Gringos, the job we got to do here is
              win the hearts and minds
         of these redskin bellyachers. Now,
         we got some good injuns—on
   a few old nickels, in front of cigar stores, and
          up here on the platform (nods
               to mannikins), but
         we got to win over the rest, show
            em what MERICA is all about—
       fireworks, democracy, and free enterprise.
       True, we got a few of em sellin neckties, and
       we got a few of em whoopin at rodeos, and
          we got a few of em busy makin curios (though
               that's strained our relations with
    Japan somewhat), and
    we got a whole *lot* of em suckin booze. But
             we got to get the rest. MERICANS,
           we got to find a practical and
         humane (but final) solution to
              the Indian Problem. So
   I'm asking you to cinch up for this challenge,
         I'm askin you to knuckle down,
       I'm askin you to serve your country
               as she's served you.

My fella MERICANS, I'm askin you
   to begin today, distasteful as it may be,
   this very afternoon I'm askin you
to find you a redskin and, yes, MERICANS,
TAKE AN INDIAN OUT TO YOUR FOURTH OF JULY PICNIC!

(George Armstrong Custer Memorial Drum
and Sousaphone Band strikes up, rising, with
   the speaker's voice, to the occasion . . .)

   That's right, MERICANS, take
one of our feathered friends out to lunch,
   let him see what AMERICA's all about.
Let him see the beauty of Old Glory,
      let him be inspired by
      the greatest story every told, Come
on now MERICANS, *everybody* SING
         OHHH SAY CAN YOU SEE
         BY THE DAWN'S EARLY LIGHT
         WHAT SO PROUDLY WE HAILED
         AT THE TWILIGHT'S LAST GLEAMING
            AND THE ROCKET'S RED GLARE . . . (at
this verse the mannikin chief begins to grind, rumble, and
      whir, coming to life
         in somber inexorable Indian fashion, the
      bulbs in his eye sockets blink, his
   limbs and torso quiver and twitch, jerky
at first, like an automaton, but
         feeling for their own rhythm and motion, his
            electronic glands produce oil and
            moisture on his skin, his
   jaws work slowly, he
         belches, farts, and burps, his alternating
            current begins
         to merge with his soul, he
speaks, halting sounds at first, then
         syllables, begins to chant, finding

76

                    his rhythm—*hi-yi-yi,*
               Everyone is amazed, the
                    Sousa band squiggles raggedly, the
                         singing falters and stops. The
                    chief speaks:
          Injuns beware / there's hostiles out there /
armed with guns, caps, and crackers / injuns beware /
     or, as Shakespeare says, /
                         Holy Toledo, Amos,
               his sword's out!
                    The speaker, recovering, is
               outraged at blasphemies
               against great music, America, Shakespeare,
     prosody, grammar, and The Radio Corporation of America.
     Mannikin Chief continues to rumble and
                    whir, continues his verse, the
               audience is agape. Speaker
has to get the audience back,
               hoarse stage whisper to assistant,
          "for Chrissake pull his plug,
                    cross his wires,
               jam his circuits, do
     *some*thin," goes after audience . . .)
               Don't you worry none about him, friends,
     just a little hitch in the programmin. But
               you see what I mean, MERICANS,
          we got us a job to do.
          That's Old Glory (gestures to flag),
     that's the Star Spangled Banner,
that's the country we love. Those
          injuns don't like it here, they
               can go back to India, right folks?
                    (audience still agape, even
          old faithful bread and
          butter routine can't get them back, speaker
               is desperate, goes

77

     into Mitch Miller sing-a-long . . .)
   Let's have a little song
friends and neighbors, a chorus of "Home on the Range,"
  yessirreebob, this is the
    spot for that, right folks?
   Maestro, if you please (Sousa band
 lurches into song, speaker waves his arms and sings)
OH GIVE ME A HOME . . . Come *on* MERICANS,
  let's *hear* it, OH GIVE ME A HOME . . . that's
   it MERICANS . . . WHERE THE BUFFALO
 ROAM . . . remember buffalo, friends and
neighbors, it's like apple pie and mom and hay rides
 and moon and june and spoon: buffalo,
  MERICANS, a fairy wonderland,
 like yesterday and tomorrow . . .
just a tourist attraction on the Old West Trail . . .
  a picture postcard for the folks back home . . .
   Now for you old timers,
    a little chorus of "Across
      the Alley from the Alamo," remember
   that one, MERICANS, that one
  was a biggie, a million seller, let's *hear* it,
ACROSS THE ALLEY FROM THE ALAMO, COME ON
  everybody join in, LIVED
    AN INDIAN PONY AND A NAVAJO / AND
THEY VERY VERY RARELY / GAVE A
   HI-DE-HO / TO THE PEOPLE
PASSIN BY . . .
   ONE DAY THEY WENT A-WALKIN /
ALONG THE RAILROAD TRACK . . . / TOOT-TOOT,
  AND THEY NEVER CAME BACK . . don't
 you worry none about the redskins, MERICANS,
 just a fairy tale, a
Disney diorama on the Old West Trail . . . marvelous,
  so life-like, they
    walk, they talk, they crawl
  on their belly like a reptile (nervous

glance at Mannikin Chief), but
don't you worry, none, MERICANS,
Toot-Toot, and they never came back . . .

whereupon, sure enough, Mannikin Chief
begins blinking and lurching, belching and
farting; searches through his computer bank again
for the right words, syllables first, *hi-yi-yi,
hoy-yoy-yoy, hi-yi-yi, hoy-yoy-yoy,* then
phrases—The FBI in Peace and War,
Mr. District Attorney, I Spy, Star Trek, Bonanza,
Red Ryder (and Little Beaver), The
Lone Ranger and his faithful Indian
Companion. "I'm
sorry I fucked up again Marshal Dillon: That's all
right, Chester, you're the best friend
a man ever had" . . . *all
hell breaks loose,* the audience
and the speaker are screaming, STOP HIM,
STOP HIM, PULL HIS PLUG, SHOOT, SHOOT, SOMEBODY SHOOT HIM!
but all the ammunition is in Cambodia, and
Mannikin Chief at last finds
his voice,
Injuns beware / there's hostiles out there . . .
hysteria: everyone screaming and shouting,
all the visiting dignitary generals
in their doorman's uniforms
are unarmed, shouting commands,
Column to the right, Harch! Column to the *right,* TO THE RIGHT!
the audience scrambles, Mannikin Chief
is moving now, and chanting,
at each step his
motion is more fluid, he grows,
more and more immense, great seven league strides,
he marches through the Lilliputian audience,
out onto the prairies,

>   the skies open up, a great deluge, he
>   scoops up a handful of mud, makes
>   an effigy of a horse, the horse
> comes alive, grows,
> Mannikin Chief mounts,
>   takes hammer and chisel in his great hands,
>   slings a huge pouch of dry powder
> over his shoulder, and
>   rides south toward the Black Hills
>   where Crazy Horse waits to be reborn . . .

IX

Song for Hairy Chin

The place is North Dakota, but the backdrop's
Byzantine. A monkey gone in silk's
a monkey still, and this gaunt man
festooned as Uncle Sam's Dakotah, known
as Hairy Chin. Top hat and tails
make the injun good, though three days later
he was better still. Back home at Standing Rock
they call him Uncle Sham. Bad medicine
will get you if you don't watch out
or even if you do. In short, it did.
This monkey aped The Man.
Down the bannered streets of Bismarck he
shuffled in parade, sporting snow white
whiskers on his chin.
Were those whiskers mutant? Was
the hatchet buried for real, or
in Sham? Let's not be facile.
Who died for Custer's sins?

For all his monkeyshines, this man's
no joke. He looks directly at
the lens, full face engraved unsmilingly
in time. Stout-hearted Gall (his pal?)
declined, but Sitting Bull joined right
in, a season with Buffalo Bill.
Bad medicine will get you if
you don't watch out or do. But
after all Gall signed, and Sitting Bull declined.
And for all the monkeyshines, there
is no joke. This monkey aped The Man,
prancing down the street, striped pants,

top hat, and tails, all red white and blue . . .
mutantly bewhiskered, his face
cadaverously thin. And then? His
days were numbered, fewer than
the fingers I use to hold my pen.
What was July Fourth to him, this
Indian with whiskers on his chin?
He strutted like a bright plumed cock.
But three days later, as owls were hooting
at Standing Rock, Coyote opened the door.
His heart went out. In the great night,
for all his monkeyshines, this man's
no joke, whose death's head addresses the lens.
Let's not be facile. Here's living proof
who died, and how, for Custer's sins.

X

Plainsong at Crowheart Butte

1

Near this place they fought, Shoshoni
and Bannock against the Crow . . . this river
basin harbored buffalo . . . today
blond boys gallop in the spring ride
herd on herefords beneath this morning's sun pale
men in Stetsons peddle hardware in
Dubois Conoco and Exxon promise antlers
for a tankful of supreme . . . near this place
they fought . . . Shoshoni and Bannock
against the Crow . . . this
river basin harbored buffalo.

And near this place the strut macabre . . . thus
suppose a moon . . . suppose it full exquisite
absolute . . . its light . . . the corpses . . . Shoshoni Bannock
Crow . . . Washakie conquering Shoshoni chief cuts
the heart from one dead Crow and
jabs it on his lance . . . suppose his rush the thrill
the killer's thrill of life the taste the salty
taste of sweat like blood damp upon his lip his
eyes *his eyes* his own heart pumping
breath into the night his veins
so flushed that they distend . . . suppose
beneath the moon he raises to its light
the skewered heart and chants, his lucid
song suffusing night like moonlight . . . far off
perhaps the Crow as well beneath indifferent
phases of the full indifferent moon, benign and
absolute, perhaps the Crow, far off, hearing

know . . . *among some tribes the custom
is to eat the heart or liver of
a worthy foe* . . . the Crow, far off, hear perhaps and
know . . . Washakie his eyes and blood aflame, chants
holding high his bloody lance and
leads the ancient dance beneath the moon
full and absolute . . . there are those perhaps
who, far off, hearing know . . . this place the
strut macabre . . . they call it Crowheart Butte . . .
here Shoshoni and Bannock fought the Crow
this river basin harbored buffalo

2

And near this place while Washakie
"displayed" a dead Crow heart and danced Jake
Astor's boys passed through unperturbed . . . John
Jacob Astor never saw Astoria still
we must suppose he was amused . . . at Washakie
his bleeding heart and strut beneath the moon . . .
Tell my man he's number one Astor
winking told his crew keep a sharp eye out for beaver
and the swivel oiled your
gatling gun will get you through . . . Oh
yes Astor said crossing silken legs and
savoring an elegant cigar We
are much amused . . . spread the word . . . today
this roadside point of interest self-interestedly
proclaims "Washakie a mighty warrior . . . a wise chief
friendly to the whites . . ." inviting tourists to
return with us to Yesteryear and his faithful
Indian companion making highways to the sea
for *in this chief's teepee* we are told
hung no white man's scalp . . . Jake Astor never
saw Astoria but the ledger

shows he was astute . . . this monument
was easy . . . the sign says Crowheart Butte.

And Washakie we must suppose was much obliged
at something so grandiose as "history"
treating him so fine . . . how
could he know he grinned a Stepnfetchit grin and
danced a soft shoe shuffle sporting
that awesome heart upon his eagle feathered lance and
singing bravely as he danced, *I
feed your heart to dogs Crow they
shit upon your grave.* Astor placed his fine cigar
between his teeth and smiled as he applauded. That boy's
good I think he can be used . . . and
"in consideration of the local chief" wise
and mighty chief supreme arbiter of this basin's
buffalo almighty shaker of a dead Crow
heart upon a stick in consideration as they say of
the local chief they call this fort
Fort Washakie . . . today with Astor's blessing
I pass blandly through this land that that
Crow's heart like Washakie's beat to have . . . and
under Astor's moon a moon so big
it bathes a continent in exquisite silver
light last night I took a leak and dumped
where willows mark both their graves . . . down the road
there is this place where Washakie was silly
while Astor was astute . . . this monument
was easy . . . they call it Crowheart Butte.

3

Moonset flight of the owl sunrise cicadas sing
Wind River in the spring
I bathe ablution in the high spring run

horses grazing ablution in the cold fast waters
thank you Bannock and Shoshoni thank you for this place
in the morning's golden sun Fort
Washakie spelled out in stones
whitewashed on the hill Fort
Washakie sanctuary to white men fugitive
from Sioux white men Sacacawea Fort
Washakie her grave Sacajewea her grave this grove
defiled my clean white body defiles
this blest indifferent grove because Sacajewea
Sacacawea Sacajewea Sacacawea because
Sealth Seattle Sealth because Joseph
Hinmaton Yahlatlat Joseph because Crazy Horse Crazy
Horse said yes the interpreter said no because
the bayonet the corporal's bayonet in his
side because Napoleon was
a corporal because Hitler was a corporal because Old
Hickory was a corporal because this
grove is real estate because Sacacawea Joseph Seattle
Captain Jack Crazy Horse Wounded Knee Sand Creek Saigon Fort
Washakie because we couldn't get the lingo or
wouldn't even E.P. thick skinned and bold let
not the daughter no nor any of us
burnish what is tarnish the sins too
will teach us because E.P. the dazzle of
sweat and coin fixed rightly in his third eye who
learned nine languages ancient and
modern east and west and knew King James
precisely for what it was collaboration
hegemony of the rich and righteous because E.P. lamenting
this half savage country couldn't get the lingo
nor the fathers of our country not
Jefferson his dictionary awash in Chesapeake Bay
not Jackson who put the Creeks in their graves and
sold the plots in Philadelphia because
not any of us could get the lingo or would because Shakespeare
maker of beauties even on the edges of civilization

     bedazzled us and John Wilkes Booth with blank verse and
            Cicero in his mouth bedazzled us because
spelled sixteen different ways Shakspeer Shakespere Shakespeare
         Shakespear he Washakie in whose tipi hung
              no white man's scalp he Washakie
    shook his spear jabbed on it the fresh heart of a dead
   Crow his enemy the Crow and danced because in celebration
    he Washakie enemy of Sioux and Crow and Nez Perce
succor (sic) of white men because killer of none he Washakie
           namesake and hero of this grove defiled wise
    and mighty chief he Washakie learned our lingo carved
          the heart of one good Crow because because
            thank you Bannock and Shoshoni thank you
         ablutions in this morning's golden sun thank you
high spring waters thank you cicadas thank you sunrise thank you
  flight of the owl thank you moonset moonset moonset because

XI

Dakotah Plainsong

Now there is no heron here,
starkly poised,
its spur uplifted
from its shadow, subtle
on the darkening stream—
No kinetic fisher waits
vertical and still
to strike, eat, stretch,
and swing above the hills—
The hills, their autumn lines,
their opulence at dusk,
deceive serenely
and belie this leaving plain
which wears
like sixty years of suet
wear away the teeth
and leave blunt stumps
in withered gums—
Weather marks
these plains,
scattering their signs
of enterprise—
the hogan of the Mandan,
the tipi of the Sioux
are splintered
through the badlands'
withering display—
For weather marks
these plains
and men
root this futile

              dirt, they
                grow
              sweetbriar
          and strawberry wire
             and sour wine,
       while the winter heron hurries
       to lily, germander, and columbine.

XII

Chiricahua Plainsong

1

Arizona Highways coordinate
    the landscape:
               even undulations help
    to make us
      manageable. . . . tanks
rolling on rubber treads, like
      Buicks, there
    and on the west side
               of Chicago. . . . "the
  fiery forges of center earth
thrust up massive mountains, table lands
and anvil-like mesas. And
    with the powerful yet delicate tools
of creation—sun, wind, water
      and timeless age on
        timeless age—there evolved
  a land of indescribable beauty . . .
        while the Declaration
was being written and
              the war for independence
    fought, Arizona
was a far-off nameless place . . .
        Now, as then, a place
    of peace and beauty."

Arizona Highways coordinate
    the landscape,
        and counties bear their names
    like tombstone plots

     coordinate with the delicate
  tools of fiery creation . . . Mohave, Yuma,
      Maricopa, Yavapai, Pima, Pinal,
   Navajo, Apache, Cochise . . . RIP.
Age on countless age
   of peace and beauty meld. . . . Like
    form & content, time
  & place, this melting pot, and
  willy-nilly we
are in a stew. Content
without form? No
   we are not prepared for that. From
   north and south and east
the lost redeemers come—El Camino Real, the
     trail to Sante Fe . . . Cortes
 & Kit Carson
bloody & body of
     humid Mediterranean
  mysteries. Peace
on earth . . . oil on troubled
    waters, not a ripple on
Lake Havasu, its smooth gleam
      silver beneath the London
  Bridge. Form
  without content? No, we are not prepared . . .
         So then,
 Ponce, as guide to Arizona Highways
  in the sky, prone
 & languid on his pony, stroking,
     indolent in
    the sun, when something
  caught his eye . . .
    "Apache! Apache!"
Feet small, pony no shoes, Apache horse go all around
   just like Apache. . . . By
this we understood Americans in contrast

                    ride straight on
                from hill to hill. And

        so does Howard. If
    war was hell and hell was hot
    he came bringing heaven to the desert, peacefully—
                one armed, unarmed on
            a bright bad day, one of many, at
                                Tularosa or
                        the Bosque Redondo.
                Coordinate: intersect
            the Chiricahuas . . . straight ahead
                    from hill to hill. . . . I'd
    give my arm
        to be the Moses of
            the Negro, he
    said. And did. His
                    mission next was Indians. That
                Christian soldier stuff is all right in its
                        place, but
            he needn't put on airs
        among ourselves. . . . He
    does all his good in such queer ways. . . . Missus
                the knees are wore
            out every pair of pants I got,
                    prayin. . . . But

            when invited he did so, dancing thus—
    on either side a
    chatty Chiricahua woman held,
                    one to his left hand, the
                other to his empty sleeve. . . . Form?
            Content? What
                    signs are these? A
            bit of cracker or sugar lump
        seduced Apache children . . . they

          nestled at my feet and
                    lay their little heads upon . . .
               what signs? And if
          Cochise's son should learn to write his name?
                    Form without content?
               Our young women will attend to your lieutenant. . . .
                    And these, he said,
               these are signs of war?

                              2

               Unarmed, deliberate as
          the destiny whose agency he is,
                                   Howard
                         reins up before the monolithic
                    Chiricahuas. Anxious
               Sladen whispers in his ear. The
                    Christian soldier
                    ponders face to face
               the sacrificial: oneself,
          one's faithful friend. . . . "Whosoever, Captain,
     will save his life shall lose it, but
          whosoever will lose his life
                         for my sake
                    the same shall save it."
               Form & content bemused
                         by paradox, Sladen shuts his yap.

          Generals Crook, Miles, and Terry are
     Spartan, big boned & bare knuckled
     obedient servants to the oldest most
                    efficient forms
          of truth. Nonetheless   there are
                         Cochise, Nana, Geronimo, names
                    children use today to conjure daring-do. So,
               the mission is

            change coordinates, intersect
                    Athens, Chiricahua, Calvary . . . "By
        God's help in Christ we
can raise men to the Beautiful and Good. . . ." Form
                        & content, content
                            & form intersect . . . Athens
                    Chiricahua, Calvary . . . old soldiers
            ponder sacrificial form . . . the
    old, efficient truths are
met in kind,
            chin to chin, or not. And
                    even Grant
                    called the simple slaughter (of
            disarmed Maricopas) simple
    slaughter. Insoluble, form & content.
            Old Soldiers
                    find such stuff
            distasteful, a black eye
                                for the trade. So,
            change coordinates. Exterminating
    angels deplore violence. It's
            inhumane. Deliver Negroes
                    from their bondage, savages from sin.
            Civilities. Stick 'em bleed 'em
                    pop 'em in the pot . . .
            melt 'em meld 'em formaldehyde
            their thought. . . . change
        coordinates, form, and
                            content. . . .   Paradox
            is the art of speaking
                        with your tongue in both
                    cheeks (whose? hmmm, only
        Moses has seen God's hinder
    parts and
            only God can make a tree
        fall in the forest today. . . . form?
content?) at the same time. By

                                                    109

                    which I mean we
                had to *destroy* the village
                                        in order to save it. Left
            to themselves Apaches don't
            have the sense God gave a flea, to
                        eat three meals a day. Even Pedro
                    who acquired manners quickly speared
                bread by fork and
            took his meat with fingers. Form
                            and content. . . Teach you
                        all I know and still you don't know
                                        nothing. But,
                when sober, Indians
                may be managed. And
            by Christ we can manage even these . . .

                        Still, as soldiers go, he
                    was one who had the / kind of guts it takes to
            dance beneath a Chiricahua
                        moon. Moreover, sugar lumps
                    seduced the shyness of Apache children. They
                        nestled at my feet . . . they
                    lay their little heads upon my
                            blanket . . . Cochise's son
                    learned from me to write his name . . . the
                        conduct of the women was
                            uniformly good . . . I
                    introduced a system of
                        three meals a day . . . the
            object of my mission was
                accomplished . . . strange ceremonies
        for consulting spirits were observed, the
                women's muffled moaning
                low in imitation of
                the wind . . . Cochise
                in mournful recitatif . . .
                which side the Styx . . . their

superstitions we did not know . . . Cochise
   in mournful recitatif . . .
  he raised his eyes
  I observed his courtesy
   his simple grace
 his mournful recitatif
shi-cowah shi-cowah shi-cowah
  These mountains / are my home

3

  Wary, high among the craggy
   Chiricahuas, deliberate as
an old ancestral king Cochise
  sees destiny approach disarmed, straight on
   from hill to hill. *Buenos Dias, Senor,*
 Though he kills ten whites for
   each Apache, still
from somewhere beyond the sea beyond
  the dawn there are whole continents indefatigable,
producing men with guns who wait implacably
  to wade ashore. *Buenos Dias, Senor* . . . may
  the son of god and light everlasting
upon whose empire and sun declines to set
   grab you by your scruffy neck and
 shove you up the ass of buffalo or antelope
  or eagle and sublimate your form, give us
   something to believe in.
   Meanwhile, Senor, I
  do not want to go to Tularosa.
The flies there eat the horses' eyes.
Buenos Dias, Senor. I have drunk these waters
  and they have cooled me. I
   do not want to go to Tularosa. He
holds his hard, lean hands before him.
Buenos Dias. Another race. Another

            time. His face is tinted
    with vermilion. His hair is straight
        and black, streaked with silver threads.
          Destiny observes the silver threads
          and smiles. Destiny's a friend
        of time. *Buenos Dias.* Cochise's shoulders
        sag. His courtesy. His simple
          grace. His wrath. Beside
      the point. Form without content. *Buenos
          Dias.* To raid the Mexicans. To
    raid the gringos. Form without
content. *Buenos Dias, Senor.* Apaches
beg indifferent skies, *come down, come down!*
    Buenos Dias, Senor. Apaches
   want to die. They carry their lives
upon their fingernails. *Buenos Dias.* I
   do not want to go to Tularosa.
      Buenos Dias. I
do not want to go to Tularosa. The
   flies there eat the horses' eyes. *Buenos
   Dias.* I do not want to go
  to Tularosa. I have drunk these
waters and they have cooled me. *Buenos
      Dias.* I do not want
        to go to Tularosa. I have
        drunk these waters *Buenos Dias* his
courtesy his simple grace beside the point . . . his
            wrath   form without his courtesy
        his simple grace pondering

      the sacrificial   the wind in the eagle's
          wing the wind among the silky
        tassels of the small corn the wind
        in my daughter's hair the morning
      star above the desert   the evening star
          above the peaks the laughter
        at the blossoming of cactus fruit the

laughter in the cactus liquor the
  laughter in the morning songs the
 dancing of the virgins on the sunbeams the
laughter in the evening songs the
  dancing of the virgins on
the long bow behind the rain the
laughter in the mountains with
 the slender rain the young girls
singing in the third dawn when
the people fall in love there singing
    with the rainbow bright before me
    with the rainbow bright behind me
    with the rainbow bright above me
    with the rainbow bright below me
 with the rainbow everywhere around me
    may I walk among the mists
  of the long bow behind the rain
      being as it used to be
    and bounty in the dark clouds
    and ripe fruit in the baskets
    and ripe fruit bringing rain
   and thunder rolling in the mountains
and when he talked to me my breath became
form without wrath pondering the sacrificial
   his courtesy his simple grace his
 courtesy his simple grace his courtesy
      Buenos Dias Buenos Dias Buenos Dias
      shi-cowah shi-cowah
    These mountains are my home . . .

XIII

"Bestride the Mighty and Heretofore Deemed Endless Missouri"

An Essay on the Corps of Discovery

1

On the eastern slope
some were brazen, bold
as brass—the
young squaws even occasionally
hustling a ride in the strange up-river
sailing ship (a curious custom with the Sioux
and as well the Pawnee, they
give handsome squaws to those whom they wish to
show some acknowledgment. The
Sioux we got clear of
without taking their squaws.
They followed us two days.
They persist in their civilities. . . .)

But once past the Divide things were different. The Shoshoni women who had no word for white man but *tab-ba-bone,* enemy, were as if prophetically afraid. Coming within 30 paces unexpectedly of three female savages, they appeared much alarmed but saw we were too near for them to escape by flight. They therefore seated themselves on the ground holding down their heads as if reconciled to die.

Sunburnt, Lewis looked to be her natural enemy, but
when he stripped his shirt, showing
his white belly she appeared, he said,
instantly reconciled.
For the instant, as he took the old woman

by the hand and raised her up
gave her beads, moccasin awls, pewter mirrors and
painted her cheeks with vermilion, which
with this nation is a sign of peace, she
was no doubt for the instant,
as he said, reconciled. Now more than ever,
though she appeared otherwise to Lewis and
perhaps herself, she
was reconciled to die.

Her men, though armed and expecting enemies, the
Minnetarees, were disarmed by these pale apparitions
bearing gifts. Embracing
fate affectionately, in their way, they
place the left arm on our right shoulder
clasping our back while
they apply their left cheek to ours, saying
ah-hi-e, ah-hi-e.
I am much pleased.
I am much rejoiced.

Then the ceremony of the pipe
the sacred pledge of friendship, barefoot,
vulnerable and exposed, honoring
three times from East to North the points of the heavens—
the stem to the earth
then to the white men
then one another. Making
as only the women seemed to know
their peace with death. . . . "Several of the old
women were crying and imploring the Great Spirit
to protect their warriors, as if they
were going to inevitable destruction."

The Corps of Discovery came in peace.
They came with blue beads.
And scarlet red vermilion.

On the western slope of the Bitteroots, as they approached the first Nez Perce village, most of the women fled to the neighboring woods with their children, a circumstance he had not expected as Captain Clark had previously been with them and informed them of our pacific intentions. The men seemed but little concerned and several came out to meet them, unarmed.

Later, as if some aboriginal players devised the scene, Broken Arm took flour from the roots of cows and thickened the soup in the kettles of all his people, inviting those who would abide by the council to come and eat and those who would not should abstain. All but one, an old man, celebrate the feast.

And outside the lodge
the women, he said, cried, wrung their hands, and
tore their hair. The women, he noted,
filled the air with lamentations. The women
with their heads bowed to receive death.
The women riding with their children to the hills.
The women
always the women
filling the air with lamentation. What,
in their fear, in their womanly weakness, in
their women's hearts, what did they know
that he, Lewis, meticulously
noted their fear and lamentation?

He told the chief, Cameahwait, he was sorry for their lack of trust. He told the chief that among white men it was considered disgraceful to lie, to entrap an enemy by falsehood . . .

(There were yet he hoped some Shoshoni
not afraid to die. Or have you all, he said,
the hearts of women, and noted
again meticulously
that he had "touched the right string."

119

No, the chief said, I am not afraid to die.
The solemnity of the pipe, then.
And the women imploring the Great Spirit
as if, he noted, they were going
to inevitable destruction . . .

Exultingly he thanked his God that he had lived to bestride the mighty and heretofore deemed endless Missouri.

2

York
the big black buck
"servant" Clark said
the way a Virginia gentleman don't say *slave* or *nigger*
don't say *shit* if he had a mouthful.

Said, "canoes of skins passed down from the two villages and many came to view us all day, much astonished at my black servant who did not lose the *opportunity* [my italics] of displaying his powers, strength &c. This nation never saw a black man before."

May be—can't say—they
never either saw a "servant" before.
Better they get used to it.
Going to see it a lot.
Going to be it. Soon enough
going to be more big
bad black curly haired bozos in Dakota
than Pawnees.

Those aborigines much astonished at my servant indeed!
York carrying on with his powers and all,
not missing the opportunity. *He*
ain't getting no medals, large *or* small size,

picture of Jefferson. . . . All
flocked around and examined him
from his nappy burr head to his two-toned
pink and black toes. *He* don't miss
no tricks. . . . carried on the joke, he said,
and made himself more terrible
than we wished him to do. Yeah,
old York coming down *bad* right there at the start.
Don't miss a trick, putting them
Pawnees on. A little show,
black boy doing honest-to-god *black face*
right there on the prairie—heart of America.
Just, God knows, a little bit
badder than we wished. But OK
a little divertisement
in the middle of the big play.

Break out the fiddle now,
show them shuck footed Pawnees some *rhythm.*
He ordered his black servant
to dance, which (naturally)
amused the crowd
much, and even somewhat astonished them
that so large a man should be active &c.
Those people are much pleased with my black servant.
And he don't miss a trick,
showing off his powers. . .

(and their women, fond of caressing . . .)
old York must of had himself a time, their
women very fond of caressing
caressing I dare say
his powers, and
his powers getting bigger by the minute
making himself more terrible than
we wished and
you can make book on it too.

Old Stepnfetchit
being *baaad* right out there beyond the frontier,
just laffin and showing off his powers . . .

    (there once was a Pawnee maid
    who said she wasn't afraid
    to lay on her back
    in a prairie shack
    and let a *black* cowboy !?
    diddle in her crack.
    And then to her surprise
    her belly began to rise . . .)

Ohhh Yassuh, Yassuh the dancer said
and then for prophecy
he ate her. Marsa Clahk, he
winks and says, you think *that's* fun,
you just waits til later.

    What history records is that he made himself more terrible than we wished.

3

    Courageous, resourceful, and enterprising they had, Jefferson knew, "the true qualifications." Though lacking "a perfect knowledge" of botany, natural history, morality, mineralogy, and astronomy, they were in the end therefore found to be more reliable, American. More importantly, they were soldiers, men of skill and discretion in the use of arms—muskets of startling accuracy, the swivel gun, menacing, solid, authority unequivocally in its sweeping range.

    And, though imperfect, they were men of their time, scientific—observant, pragmatic, detached . . . enabling them to record flora, fauna, topography and native customs without prejudice (those people, Clark noted, are dirty, kind, poor, and extravagant, possessing national pride, not beggarly, receive what is given with great pleasure, live in warm houses, large, octagonal, forming a cone at the top left open for the smoke to pass, covered with earth on poles—willows and grass prevent the earth passing through. Those people express an inclination to be at peace with all nations.

Meanwhile, we tried the prisoner Newman last night by nine of his peers. They "did sentence him 75 lashes and disbanded from the party." The punishment of this day alarmed the chief very much. He cried aloud, or affected to cry. I explained the cause of the punishment and the necessity for it. He also thought examples were necessary, and he himself had made them by death. His nation never whipped even their children, from their birth.

(Note: the Arikaras are not fond of spiritous liquors, nor do they appear to be fond of receiving any or thankful for it. They say we are not friends or we would not give them what makes them fools. Those people express an inclination to be at peace with all nations.)

Also, they were practical and canny in matters of defense, enabling them to succeed where others failed—knowing only too well that *the treachery of the aborigines of America and the too great confidence of our countrymen in their sincerity and friendship has caused the destruction of many hundreds of us.* Those people express an inclination to be at peace with all nations.

Then too they were men exemplary not only in their skills but also in their morals, inspiring loyalty and discipline in the field. On Christmas Eve a Clatsop chief offered a woman to each of them, which they declined accepting of, and displeased the whole party very much, the female part, especially. This was the same party which had communicated the venereal to several of our party in November last. I therefore gave the men a particular charge with respect to them, which they promised me to observe. Old Dlashelwilt and his women still remain, but I believe, notwithstanding every effort of their winning graces, the men have preserved their constancy to the vow of celibacy which they made on this occasion to Captain Clark and myself.

No wonder, then, that they should fulfill their president's charge—to ascend the Missouri to its source, to cross the Highlands, to locate and follow the best waterway from thence to the Pacific Ocean, to establish friendly contact with the aborigines, to assert thereupon the power of the White Father over their trade, comfort, and well being, to make vocabularies of native languages, to make maps, chart geography, collect horticultural, botanical, zoological, and anthropological specimens, and "as indeed they did" make way for a prosperous commerce.

Courageous, resourceful, and enterprising, they knew, meticulously and instinctively, how to touch the right strings. Though lacking a perfect knowledge, they were in the end found therefore to be more reliable, American. The fruit of America. American. Those people always expressed an inclination to be at peace with all nations.

4

From the beginning they
were received with curiosity, and
nothing more whetted interest in their mission than
an exhibit of musketry and cannon. Which
they did regularly and with great effect. Always
of course advising that
the new White Father in Washington, he
who had bought them from the anarchists
of France, he who had bought them from the
monarchists of Spain, he
the White Father

who brought them the Word, he
desired to live and trade in peace with the aborigines.
And he, they said with what sense of irony we
do not know, he desired that
they live with one another so.

(*Look back, they told Little Crow, the
Mandan war chief, with*
*what sense of irony we do not know, look
back at the number of nations who have been destroyed by war.
Reflect, they said, on what you are about to do.
If he wished the happiness of his nation he
would be at peace with all. By
that, by being at peace, and
having plenty of goods, and a free intercourse with
those defenseless nations, they
would get, on easy terms, a
greater number of horses . . . if
he went to war, he
would displease his Great Father, and
would not receive that protection and care, as
other nations who listened to his word.*
Happiness, horses, easy terms, *they said.*
Listen to his word.)

    Among the Mandan they thought it well to aid and assist them against their enemies, particularly those who came in opposition to their councils. If the Sioux were coming to attack, to collect the warriors and meet them. The chief said the village was very thankful for the fatherly protection, that the village had been crying all the night and day for the death of the brave young man who fell, but now they would wipe away their tears and cry no more.

Rejoice, they said.
Listen to his word.

Among the Wallawallas several diseased persons requesting medical aid, to all of which we administered, much to the gratification of those poor wretches. We gave them eye-water. *It would, Clark said, render them more essential service than any other article we had it in our power to bestow.* A little before sunset the Chymnappos joined the Wallawallas and formed a half circle around our camp, where they waited very patiently to see our party dance. The fiddle was played and the men amused themselves with dancing about an hour. They were much pleased at the dancing of our men. I ordered my black servant to dance, which amused the crowd very much, and somewhat astonished them that so large a man should be active &c. They then requested the Indians to dance, which they very cheerfully complied with. They continued until ten at night. Accordingly took leave of these friendly, honest people.

Among the Nez Perce, a reception more equivocal. Here too we dispensed eyewash and liniment, gaining for our medicine, as Clark said, an exalted opinion (in our present situation, I think it pardonable to continue this deception. . . . *We take care to give them no article which can possibly injure them.*)

At dinner however
an Indian fellow very impertinently threw
a poor, half starved puppy nearly
into my plate by way of
derision for our eating dogs, and
laughed very heartily at his impertinence. I
was so provoked at his insolence that
I caught the puppy and threw it
with great violence at him and
struck him in the breast and face, seized
my tomahawk and
showed him by signs, if he repeated his insolence
I would tomahawk him . . .

> *(thereafter, he—Lewis—notes*
> *the suggestions of an old man who*
> *observed to the natives that*
> *he thought we were bad men and*
> *had come, most probably,*
> *in order to kill them . . .*

So, as all the principal chiefs were present, they thought it advisable to enter more minutely into the views of our government, its plans for the natives of this western continent, its intention of establishing trading houses for their relief, its wish to restore peace and harmony, above all the strength, power, and wealth of our nation, their well being at the disposal of its will, &c. Then, they amused themselves with demonstrating the power of magnetism, the spyglass, compass, watch, air gun, and sundry other articles equally novel and incomprehensible to the savages.

> (still, in his journal, the
> record of what the old man thought and said,
> that we were bad men and had come, most
> probably, in order to kill . . .

After we had eaten a few roots, we spoke to them and gave each a medal of the small size with the likeness of Mr. Jefferson, and to some the sowing medals struck in the presidency of Washington. We explained to them the design and importance of medals in the estimation of whites, and as well the red men who had been taught their value.

> (still, in his journal, the old man . . .

The Nez Perce held a council on the morning of the 18th.
They resolved to listen to his word.
Then Broken Arm, the chief, took

flour from the roots of cows and
thickened the soup in the kettles of all his people.
He made a harangue, impressing
the need for unanimity. . . .
Happiness, horses, and easy terms.
They listened to his word.

Meanwhile he—Lewis—scrupulously
reported, outside the lodge the women
cried, wrung their hands, and tore their hair, as
if, he said, they
were going to inevitable destruction.
And the old man
the old man said we were bad men, bad
men who had come, most
probably, to kill . . . . *And the women, he
recorded, cried
and tore, he said, their hair.*

5

Having himself lived to watch
McNeal straddle the creek and
thank his God that he had lived to
bestride the mighty and heretofore deemed endless
Missouri, he—Lewis—noted, the
evening of August 18, that
he had this day completed his thirty-first
year. (He
>spent the day in commerce, bartering a uniform
>coat, a pair of leggings, a few handkerchiefs,
>three knives and some other small things "the
>whole of which did not cost more than about $20
>in the United States" for three "very good
>horses" from the Shoshoni.)

Having, though he did not know it,
completed about half of his expedition and
nearly all of his life, he
conceived that he had "in
all human probability now existed
about half the period which I am to
remain in this sublunary world." As
always, in consciousness and style, he
was a man of his age and did not, like McNeal,
thank his God but spoke grandly of
sublunary contrition. He
reflected that he had as yet done
but little, very little, to
further the happiness of the human race, or
to advance the information of
succeeding generations. But,
as yet a man of his rotarian age, he
dismissed that gloomy past and
resolved in future to redouble his exertions
and at least endeavor to promote those two
primary objects of human existence—to
live *for mankind,* as
he had heretofore lived *for himself.*
A man of his age.
On occasion grand and grandly spoken.
On occasion gloomy and alone,
pacing, while others sailed, the shore.
Alone of that resourceful, courageous, and
enterprising band, the
fruit of destiny's own breed,
Lewis alone of those
recorded the women and the old man.
Lewis, the moody, the solitary,
perhaps four years later the suicide.

An old Nez Perce man, he said,
who thought they were bad men and
had come, most probably, in order to kill.
And the women, who cried
and wrung, he said, their hands and
tore, he said, their hair.
Lewis alone recorded the women and the old man.

Lewis, who made the savages sensible
of their dependence on the will of our government for
every species of merchandise as
well for their defense and comfort.
Lewis, who took care to give the children
of the White Father no article which
could possibly injure them. Lewis,
who dispensed medals of large and small size.
Lewis, who with his medicine, his weapons, his
audacity, his ambition, his genius incarnated
the spirit and power of his country . . . this
same Lewis remarks the old man's prophecy and
that the women wailed.
Did he reflect, for all
that he advanced the information of succeeding
generations, did he reflect on his
resolve to live for mankind, did he, four
years later at Grinder's Stand on the Natchez
Trace, did he, reflecting, know
as he morosely squeezed the trigger
finger of his always disciplined hand, did
he know, remembering his trek through the savage
sublunary world, did he know,
remembering the women and the old man, did he,
at the fulcrum of past and future,
scanning as a haunted man dark horizons in
that dark night, did he
see and seeing know, whoever
triggered his long night dying, did he

know precisely, having traveled to its far edge
and back, did he know, as
he cut his biography in half, did
he know precisely why and what he, reliable
American that he was, had done?

The Corps of Discovery came in peace
bearing the word, blue beads,
and scarlet red vermilion.

    6

For that we were no scholars
and lacking a perfect knowledge we
were found to be more reliable, American.
We followed absolute as mortal man can do
our high command. And
we came, as the old man said,
crudely calculating probabilities, as
the old man said and Lewis strangely noted,
we, the fathers of our sons, the
sons of our fathers, were
bad men and we came, most probably, to kill.

For coming without knowledge of what we did
we were bad men. For
pacifying the Nez Perce with eyewash, liniment, and
laudenum we were bad men.
For thinking we came in peace we
were bad men. For bringing Virginia manners
to the Nez Perce we were bad men.
For our courage we were bad men.
For our strength we were bad men.
For failing to know the probability of our being
bad men we were bad men. For
bringing the badness of men to our fellow man

in the service of our country
we were bad men. We
were bad men, as the old man said, bad
men who came, *knowing well that the treachery*
of the aborigines of America and
the too great confidence of our
countrymen in their sincerity and friendship has
caused the destruction of many hundreds of us, and
we came, by any historical calculations, we
came most probably, whatever we supposed, we
came, as our leader's journal remains
to remind us, we came most probably in
order and well prepared to kill.

Accordingly, we took our leave
of these friendly, honest people.

Born in Chicago and raised in Seattle, Peter Michelson has spent considerable time in the country between those places. Two previous books, *The Aesthetics of Pornography* and *The Eater,* were published in 1971 and 1972. *When the Revolution Really* was published in 1984. A past editor of the *Chicago Review,* he is currently a contributing editor to *TriQuarterly.* His poems and essays have appeared in several anthologies and a variety of magazines, ranging from *The New Republic* to *Oink.* He has taught at Notre Dame, Northwestern, and, presently, at the University of Colorado, Boulder.